Core Knowledge Language Arts®

The Job Hunt
Unit 4 Reader

Skills Strand
GRADE 2

Amplify learning.

Core Knowledge®

ISBN 978-1-61700-210-6

Printed in the USA
NA05 LSCOW 2017

Table of Contents
The Job Hunt
Unit 4 Reader

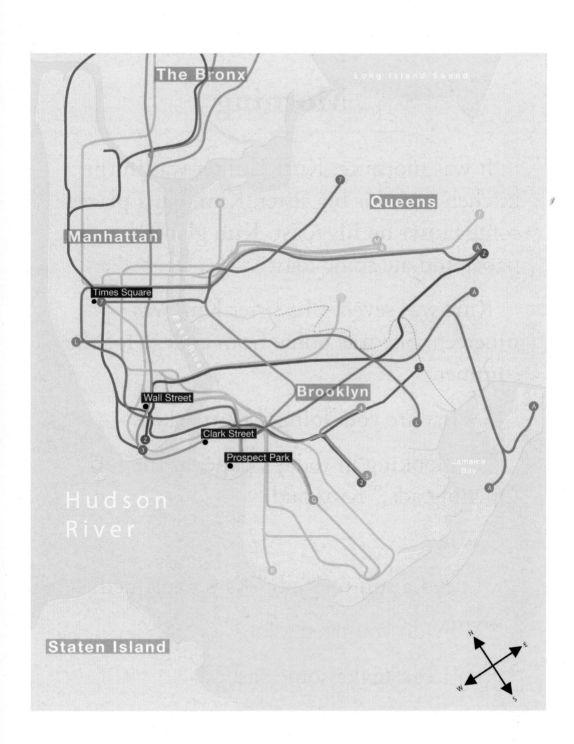

The Bronx

Long Island Sound

Queens

Manhattan

Times Square

East River

Wall Street

Clark Street

Brooklyn

Prospect Park

Jamaica Bay

Hudson River

Staten Island

Morning

It was morning. Kurt Gunter was in the kitchen with his big sister, Kim. Kurt placed some butter on his toast. Kim glanced at the paper and ate some toast.

Kurt was seven. His sister Kim was nineteen. She was home from college for the summer.

"What are you doing?" Kurt asked.

"I'm looking in today's paper at the Job Opening ads," Kim said.

"Why?"

"I need a summer job," Kim explained.

"Why do you need a job?"

"So I can make some cash."

"What will you do with your cash?" asked Kurt.

"I'll save most of it," said Kim. "But I'll spend some on things I need, like clothing. And I would like to get a bike."

"You can get a bike if you get a job?"

"Yes."

Kurt sat thinking of how much fun it would be to ride bikes with Kim.

"Cool! So, what sort of job will you get?" Kurt asked.

"I can't tell. That's why I'm looking at the paper."

Kurt ate some toast. Then he asked, "Should I get a job, too?"

Kim smiled. "You are just seven," she said. "You don't need to get a job yet. You should be having fun."

"But I would like one!" Kurt wailed.

"I'll tell you what," Kim said. "You can help me look for a job. If you see a job you like, then you can get that job when you are my age."

"That sounds good!" Kurt said.

When she finished reading the ads, Kim went and got dressed. She dressed in her best slacks and a crisp white shirt.

"Why are you all dressed up?" asked Kurt.

"It helps to dress up when you go looking for a job," Kim explained.

"Should I dress up, too?"

"Just slip on a pair of nice shorts," she told him.

Kurt ran off and got a pair of shorts.

"Would you say this pair of shorts is nice?" he asked.

"Those will do," said Kim.

Then Kim went to see her mom.

"All set for the job hunt?" Mrs. Gunter asked with a smile.

Kim nodded.

"You look nice. Did you check to see if it will rain?"

"It's not going to rain, but it's going to be hot."

"Okay. Here's a fare card for the subway," said Mrs. Gunter. "And here's some cash to pay for lunch and snacks. Call me if there's a problem."

"Thanks, Mom," Kim said.

Kurt burst into the room. "Mom, I'm going to get a job, too!" he shouted.

Mrs. Gunter said, "Your job is first to do what Kim says and then to be good while she looks for a job."

"Yes, Mom," said Kurt.

Then Mrs. Gunter spoke to Kim. "Keep your chin up. Use your best manners. Smile. And let them see how smart you are. That will help you get a job."

As they went out, Kurt asked, "Where are we going?"

Kim said, "Just stay with me."

Brooklyn

Kim took Kurt by the hand and the two of them set off so that Kim could look for a job.

It was a summer morning in Brooklyn. There were lots of cars on the streets. There were people walking here and there. A man was sweeping the street outside his shop.

Kim and Kurt walked until they got to Prospect Park.

Kurt looked into the park as they went past. He saw people playing frisbee. He saw people on bikes. He saw a man playing fetch with his dog. He saw soccer players on their way to a game. He saw runners on their way to the gym.

"Can we stop and play?" asked Kurt.

"No," Kim said. "I have to get a job."

Kurt slumped a bit to let Kim see that he was sad, but he kept walking.

"Kim," he said after a bit, "will having a job make you a grownup?"

"Well, sort of," said Kim. "I'm in college. I think that makes me part kid and part grownup."

"Will you still have time to play with me?"

"Yes!" Kim said, rubbing Kurt's arm. "We will have lots of time to play. I'll get a part-time job, one that is not too hard. That way, I will not be too tired when I get home. Then we can play."

"You should get a job at the Bronx Zoo!" Kurt said. "Then you can play with the snakes and tigers."

Kim said. "I don't think so. I don't like snakes. But we can visit the zoo later this summer. After I get a job, I will have cash to do fun things like that."

Just then Kim saw two old pals waving at her.

"Lynn!" she yelled. "Sheryl! What's up?"

Lynn and Sheryl crossed the street. "Hi, Kim!" said Lynn. "Are you home from college for the summer?"

"Yes," said Kim. "It's good to be back here in Brooklyn!"

Kim slapped hands with her pals. Then she said, "You two have met Kurt, haven't you?"

Lynn and Sheryl nodded. Lynn stooped down to look at Kurt and said, "Hi, big man! Would you like to come with us? We are going over to Drummer's Grove to see the drummers."

"Drummer's Grove?" Kurt said. "Can we go, Kim? Can we? Can we? Can we?"

Kim hesitated. She needed to get started on her job hunt. But she wanted Kurt to have fun, too. If she dragged him off without seeing the drummers, there was a chance he would get mad and fuss all day. That would not be much fun.

"Okay," she said at last. "But just for a bit. I need to get started with my job hunt."

Drummer's Grove

Brooklyn was home to all kinds of sounds. Kim and Kurt were used to lots of them. There were the sounds of traffic. Cars and trucks and buses went zipping by all the time, honking their horns and playing loud music on their sound systems. There were also the sounds of voices—people shouting and chatting and singing. There were dogs barking and even the sounds of tools that people used as part of their jobs—like a jackhammer digging a hole in the street.

This day, Kim and Kurt were soaking up the sounds in Drummer's Grove with Kim's pals, Lynn and Sheryl. Drummer's Grove is a place in Prospect Park where people gather to play drums. Some of them play steel drums. Some play bongo drums. Some of them hit the drums with sticks. Some of them slap the drums with their bare hands.

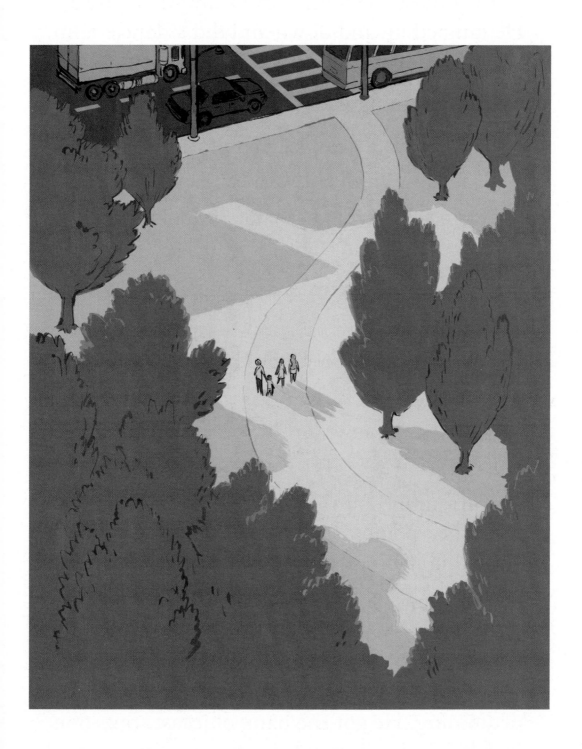

Kurt liked the sounds in Drummer's Grove. He jumped up and down and did a dance. Kim, Lynn, and Sheryl all smiled.

"Is drumming a job?" Kurt asked Kim.

"It is for some people," Kim said. "But here I think they drum just for fun."

"I can see why," Kurt said. "It looks like a lot of fun!"

"Would you like to take a shot at it?" Lynn asked.

"Do you think they would let me play?" asked Kurt.

"You won't know unless you ask," said Kim. "All they can say is no."

Kurt jumped at the chance. He went up to a drummer, pointed at his drum and said, "Would you mind if I took a turn to play?"

The drummer was kind and let Kurt have a chance. Kurt pounded on the drum and tapped his foot like he was going wild! He did his best to keep up with the rest of the drummers. He liked drumming. He got the hang of it fast. But soon he felt pain in his hands from pounding so much.

"Thanks," Kurt told the man as he gave him back the drum, "but you had better take the drum back. It's hard on my hands."

"If you do it a lot, your hands will get used to it," the drummer told him.

Kurt went back to where Kim, Lynn, and Sheryl were standing.

"You are a good drummer," Lynn told him.

"Tell Kim to get you a drum as a gift after she gets a job!" said Sheryl.

"If we don't get going soon, I'll never find a job!" said Kim. "Let's go, Kurt."

"Good luck with your job hunt," Lynn said.

"See you later!" Kim said. She waved to Lynn and Sheryl. Kurt waved to the drummers.

Dwight's Lights

Kim and Kurt walked down the street.

Kurt stopped to look at a poster.

Kim yanked on his arm. "Let's go," she said. "We can't stop till I find myself a job!"

Kim spotted the poster. It was hanging in a shop named Dwight's Lights. In big, bold letters, it said **"Dwight is hiring!"**

Kim led Kurt into the shop.

Inside the shop there were hundreds of lights and lamps. And all of them were on.

"Yikes," said Kurt, "it's bright in here!"

Just then a man came charging up. He had a big smile and a necktie with a light bulb on it. He started shouting at Kim and Kurt.

"Yes!" said the man. **"It's bright at Dwight's Lights! In fact, it's never night at Dwight's Lights! Dwight likes it bright! I'm Dwight! Yes, I am the Man of Light! Dwight's got big lights! Dwight's got small lights! Dwight's got tall lights! Dwight's got short lights! Dwight's got bright lights and brighter lights! Dwight's got lights that shut off when you clap your hands! Dwight sells all kinds of light—except sunlight. Har, har, har!"**

The man seemed to think this was the best joke of all time. But still he did not stop shouting.

"Yes, Dwight's lights are out of sight. And Dwight's price is without fail the right price! So don't think twice! Get a light at Dwight's! Yes, Miss, if you need a lamp or a light for your dorm room, you came to the right place! It's Dwight's place!"

At last the man stopped for a gulp of air.

"Um," said Kim. "I don't need a light. I just need a job. I saw the poster outside. Are you still hiring?"

When Kim said, "I don't need a light," the man's face fell and he let out a sigh.

"Job?" he said, shifting into a quiet voice. "We filled the job. Is the poster still up?" He looked at the poster.

"We should have taken this poster down," he said. "The job opening was filled last week." Then he walked off.

Kim and Kurt went back out.

"Kim," said Kurt, "Dwight was an odd man."

"Indeed, he was," said Kim.

Kurt did a bit of thinking. Then he said, "I think perhaps it's best that you did not get that job."

"I think you might be right," said Kim.

The Gym

After leaving Dwight's Lights, Kim stopped for a moment to think about where she should try next to find a job.

"Mom's pals, Tom and Beth, run a gym that is nearby. I might have a chance getting a job at their gym, so let's go!"

On the way to the gym, Kim explained to Kurt that a gym is a place where people go to exercise and get in shape. She explained that people pay to be members of a gym.

Kurt had never visited a gym. The gym seemed odd to him. He stood staring at a man who was jogging in place.

"He keeps running," said Kurt, "but he is still in the same place!"

"It's kind of like the wheel that rat of yours likes to run on," said Kim. "It lets him run in place."

"He's not a rat," said Kurt. "He's a hamster!"

Kurt kept on looking at the man jogging in place.

"Why not just run in the park?" he asked.

"Some people think the gym is fun, just like you think the park is fun," Kim said.

"All the people here are working hard," Kurt said. "Why do they pay to work so hard?"

"It makes them feel good and strong after they have finished," Kim said.

Just then Tom and Beth came over to see them.

"Hi, Kim! Hi, Kurt!" said Beth. "It's good to see you. What brings you here?"

Kim said, "I'm looking for a summer job. I stopped to see if you need help. Are you hiring?"

"We just hired someone for a job in the snack bar," Beth said, pointing over to the counter. "People like to have a cool drink and a snack when they finish in the gym."

"That looks like a good job," said Kim. "I wish I had gotten here sooner."

"Bad timing," said Beth. "We don't need more help right now. But you will find a job somewhere else."

Tom took Kurt and Kim to see the rest of the gym.

Kurt pointed at a man who was doing curls.

"What's he doing?" Kurt asked.

"He's doing curls," Tom explained. "Would you like to do some curls?"

Kurt nodded.

"Here," Tom said.

"Use this one. Lift it up. That will strengthen your biceps—the tops of your arms. Then let it down. That will strengthen your triceps—the backs of your arms."

Kurt did five or six curls. Then he clenched his arm and yelled, "I am the man of steel!"

Kim just smiled at Kurt.

Kim spoke to Beth and Tom. "Well, I suppose we should go," she said. "Thank you for meeting with me."

"No problem," said Tom.

"Good luck with the job hunt," said Beth. "We will send word to you if we need help here."

"Why don't you go see Alberto at the corner market?" added Tom. "He may have a job for you. Plus, he's one of the nicest men I ever met."

The Corner Market

"Can we quit looking for a job and go back to the park to see the drummers?" Kurt asked.

"Are you kidding?" Kim said. "I just started looking. And you know what Mom says: A winner never quits, and a quitter never wins. The corner market is just up the block. Let's try them and see if they have a job for me."

Kurt and Kim found the corner market. A bell rang as they went inside. There were all kinds of things for sale in the market. The walls and shelves were jammed with boxes and bags and cans.

"May I help you?" asked the man at the counter. He was a nice-looking man with gray hair and glasses. He spoke with an accent.

"Are you Alberto?" asked Kim.

"Yes, I am."

"Nice to meet you," said Kim. She shook his hand. "I'm trying to find a summer job. Beth and Tom at the gym suggested that I come to see you."

"I wish I had a job for you," Alberto said with a shrug. "You seem like a nice kid. But it is bad timing. I just hired someone last week. But I'll keep you in mind for the next time."

"Okay," said Kim. "Would you call me if something opens up? My name and number are written on this card."

Kim was all set to go. Then she felt a tug on her arm.

"Kim," said Kurt, "all this job hunting is tiring me out. I could use a snack."

"Okay," said Kim. "What would you like?"

Kurt said, "I would like a lime gelato."

Kim paid Alberto for the gelato.

"I was hoping *you* might pay *me*," Kim said to Alberto with a smile. "But look how things ended up—with *me* paying *you*!"

The man smiled and handed Kim some coins in return.

The Diner

The next place Kim went to look for a job was a diner.

"I'll just drop off my name and number and then we can go on to the next place," she said.

"No, no," said Kurt. "I don't think you should do that."

"Why not?" said Kim.

"You would not like to take a job in a diner without tasting the food to find out if it's good."

"Hmmm. I think that you would like to test the food at the diner, Mister Gelato!"

Kurt nodded.

They went in. The place was packed. All the booths were taken. There were people sitting on most of the stools. A waitress passed by with a huge tray piled high with dishes. It was quite a sight.

"There's a spot at the counter over there," said Kim. "Let's grab it."

Kurt and Kim waited. After five minutes a waitress came by.

"Hi," said Kim. "I would like to ask if you are hiring."

"And I would like to ask if the milkshakes here are good," said Kurt.

"You won't find a better milkshake in all of Brooklyn," said the waitress. "Would you like to try one?"

Kurt nodded. He ordered a hot dog, fries, and a milkshake.

"I'll just have coffee and pancakes," said Kim.

"Okay," said the waitress. "I'll check with the boss to see if he's hiring."

"Did you just order pancakes for lunch?" Kurt asked.

Kim nodded.

"That seems odd," said Kurt.

"No, it's not," said Kim. "You can get pancakes all day long in a diner."

"If you say so," said Kurt.

"So, what kinds of jobs do they have in a diner?" Kurt asked.

"They have the waiters and waitresses. They take orders and bring food," Kim explained. "There are people back in the kitchen, too. There is a cook and someone to clean the dishes."

The boss came over. "So, you would like a summer job?" he asked Kim.

"Yes."

"Can you cook?" he asked. "I need a cook in the morning. And I need someone to clean dishes at night."

"I'm not going to lie," Kim told the man. "I'm not the best cook. But I don't mind cleaning dishes."

"Well, to clean dishes, you would stay until midnight or one a.m. sometimes."

"That's late for me," said Kim. "That might not be the best job for me. But thank you for your time."

"Thank you, too," said the boss.

The Subway

When Kim and Kurt were finished eating, Kim paid for the meal and left a tip for the waitress. Then they went out of the diner.

"We need to get on the subway and go into Manhattan," she said.

"Manhattan?" Kurt said with a loud sigh. "This job hunt will take all day!"

"It won't take that long. I'm just having no luck here in Brooklyn. Maybe I can find a job in Manhattan."

They walked to the subway stop.

Kim got out the fare card her mom had given her.

"Which train will we take?" Kurt asked.

"The Number 3 train."

Kim pointed to a map on the wall. She showed Kurt a red line on the map. "We will ride from here in Brooklyn over to Manhattan and all the way up to Times Square."

Kurt pointed at the spot on the map that marked the East River.

"Will we get to see the river?"

"No," said Kim. "The subway goes under the river. That's why it's named a subway. Sub means under. A subway is a train that goes under things like rivers and roads. It travels underground."

Kurt and Kim waited on the platform for the subway train. Soon, Kurt could hear the sound of the train as it got closer. There was a gust of air. The train rolled up to the platform and stopped.

The people inside the subway train were packed in tight. There were no seats, so Kim reached up and grabbed a strap. Kurt held on tight to Kim's leg.

The train started off with a jerk. All the people swayed from side to side. Kurt could hear the train squeaking and creaking.

Soon, the train slowed down. A voice came over the speaker, "This is Clark Street. Next stop is Wall Street."

"Where are we?" Kurt asked Kim.

"This is the last stop in Brooklyn," Kim explained. "Next, the subway crosses over to Manhattan."

"Then can we get off? I'm so squashed I'm having a hard time breathing."

"Hang in there," Kim said. "Some people will get off as soon as we get to Manhattan."

Kim was right. The next stop was Wall Street. Lots of people got off the train.

At last, Kurt and Kim got seats on the train.

"This is much better!" Kurt said.

Wall Street

At the Wall Street stop a man got on the train. He had on black pants, a black jacket, a crisp white shirt, and a red necktie. He was holding a black case. He looked sharp.

Kurt jabbed Kim with his elbow and whispered, "What do you think his job is? Do you think he is a spy or a secret agent?"

"I don't know," Kim said. "He might be a banker who has a job in a bank on Wall Street."

"What's a bank?"

"A bank is a place where you can keep your cash so it is safe. The bank keeps your cash until you need it and they pay you a bit for saving your cash with them. Since not everyone needs their cash at the same time, the bank has extra cash that they can use to make loans to people who need cash."

"What's a loan?"

"When you get a loan from a bank, the bank lets you borrow some of the cash that it has, and you make a deal to pay the cash back later, plus some fees that the bank adds in."

"You mean you have to pay back more cash than the cash you borrow?"

"That's right."

"Why not just use the cash you've got?" Kurt asked.

"Well, if you have a lot of cash, you might not need to get a loan. But let's say you plan to open your own store. You would need a lot of cash before you even opened the store! You might not have all of this cash on your own, so you might need a loan to get started."

Kurt dreamed of a store he might like to open and of a banker handing him a big bag of cash. Then he dreamed that he might even like to be a banker himself.

"Do bankers get paid a lot?" Kurt asked.

"Some of them do."

"So why don't you get a job at a bank?"

"Most banks won't hire you unless you have finished two or three years of college. I have just finished one year."

"So it's a hard job to get?"

Kim nodded.

The Daydream

The subway train went on past Wall Street, going north.

Kim looked at the Job Opening ads in the paper.

Kurt looked up at the posters that were hanging on the walls of the train. One of them was a poster of two star baseball players. The players seemed to smile down at Kurt, as if to say, "This is the life, man!"

Kurt stared at the poster and daydreamed. He could hear a man speaking. The man was calling out the play-by-play for a baseball game.

"Two out in the ninth inning," the man said. "The home team is down by two runs. So, Mark, it looks like it's all up to Kurt Gunter at this point."

"Well, James," said a different voice, "Kurt Gunter has had such a good year. As you know, the former spaceship pilot and race car driver is leading the team in hits, home runs, and runs batted in. He has hit the ball so well this year that most fans I've spoken with think he's the bee's knees! In fact, I had a caller on my show, Sports Yap, last week who told me he thinks Gunter should make twice what they pay him."

"So Gunter steps up to the plate. Here's the pitch. It's a strike. The fans are mad. They don't like the call. They think it was a ball. But Gunter himself seems not to mind. He steps back into the box. Here's the pitch. Gunter swings."

Smack!

"Look out, Mark! He got a bit of that one! It's a long fly ball to the left. It's going, it's going. It's out of here! Kurt Gunter has hit a home run! Home run by Gunter! We win! We win!"

"James, I'm telling you, that's why Kurt Gunter is a rich man!"

"Gunter is rounding the bases. He tips his hat to the fans. The fans are going wild! They are shouting, 'Kurt! Kurt! Kurt!'"

Just then Kurt looked up. Kim was shaking him and saying, "Kurt, Kurt, Kurt! This is our stop!"

The Florist

Kim led Kurt up the stairs from the subway underground to the street.

Kurt was tired from his subway ride, but the sights and sounds of Manhattan woke him up.

He sensed the rush of hundreds of cars and trucks. He looked up at the tall buildings. Some of the tallest skyscrapers seemed to stretch up to the clouds. He looked at the throngs of people on the streets.

Kim grabbed his hand and led him down the street.

"Let's go," Kim said. "I told the florist I would be there by two."

Soon they reached the florist shop.

The shop owner was thin, old, and had gray hair. She did not smile.

She said, "My name is Hester. I own this shop." She had a mean look on her face.

"Hi, I'm Kim. The ad in the paper says you are hiring a helper."

"You got that right," said Hester. "Have you ever had a job ringing up people and taking their cash?"

"No, but I think I would be good at it. I'm good at math!"

"Have you ever had a job at a florist shop?" Hester asked.

"No. But it sounds like fun."

"Can you tell larkspur from aster?"

"No, but you could teach me."

"Is it your lifelong dream to have a job as a florist?" Hester asked.

"Well, I don't think so," said Kim. "At this point, I don't know what I want to do for the rest of my life. I'm just trying to find a summer job. Then I will go back to college in the fall."

Old Hester sighed.

"Well, that was the wrong thing to say," she said. "I need someone who will stay. You may be bright. But I won't hire someone who will leave at the end of summer."

"Okay. Thank you for your time!" said Kim with a cheerful voice.

Later, when they were back outside, Kurt said, "That florist was kind of mean."

"At least I know that's not the right job for me!" Kim said.

The Bakery

Kurt followed Kim as they made their way down the street, checking in all the shops. Then he saw something way up high.

"Look at him!" Kurt said, pointing up at a store. There was a window cleaner high up on the side and he sat on a platform. The platform was hanging by long ropes.

"He clearly has no fear of high places," said Kim. "That is not the job for me."

"I think it would be fun," said Kurt. "Think of all the stuff you could see from way up there!"

"I would rather see the sights from inside the store," Kim said. "Let's keep going. It's getting late."

Suddenly, Kurt smelled something that made his tummy thunder. The smell of freshly baked goods filled the air.

"We must go in there!" Kurt said.

It was a bakery. The baked goods were displayed in a big glass case. There were cakes and cupcakes. There were rolls and muffins. There were sticky buns and other yummy treats.

Kim asked if they had a job opening.

"Maybe," said the baker. "The boss is out. Fill out these forms. She will call you later if she has a job."

"This place is making me hungry," Kurt said.

"Here, you can have this muffin," said the baker. "It's a day old, but it's perfectly fine. It's a cranberry muffin."

Kurt bit into the muffin. "It's so tasty!" he said. "It's tart, but also sweet. What's in it?"

"All muffins start out with the same basic recipe," the man said. "You need flour, eggs, cream, and butter. The tart taste is from the cranberry. That's all I can tell you! The rest of the recipe is a secret."

"Why is it a secret?" Kurt asked.

"If I told people how to make muffins like that one, then they would not need to come here to get one."

As they left the bakery, Kurt whispered to Kim, "If you get a job here, maybe they'll teach you the secret recipe. Then we can open our own bakery."

"So you are going to be a baker now?" Kim said with a smile. "You are quite a dreamer, Kurt."

Keeping It Up

"Where to next?" asked Kurt.

"Let's just go and see what we find," Kim said.

They passed a place called Jack's Auto Shop. It was a loud place. There were men banging and drilling. One man in the auto shop was lying under a car. One man was looking under the hood of a cab.

"Do you think you can get a job in there?" asked Kurt.

"No way," Kim said. "I can't fix cars."

"I think it looks like my kind of job," said Kurt. "You get to use lots of cool tools. And you get to mess up your clothing with grease! That's perfect!"

As they went on they passed lots of carts selling food.

One of the cart men was selling roasted peanuts.

Kurt caught a whiff of the spicy peanuts and started tugging on Kim's blouse.

"Those nuts smell so good!" he said. "Can I have some?"

"Kurt!" Kim exclaimed. "You just had a cranberry muffin from the bakery!"

"But I need a snack for energy!"

"Fine," Kim said. She got Kurt some peanuts.

Kim went into a music shop. The music in the shop was so loud she had to scream, "Do you have a job opening?"

The boss yelled no.

Kim tried a clothing shop. There were no jobs.

She spoke to the owner of a bookstore. He was not hiring.

She went into a shop that sold baby clothing. "We can't help you," said the ladies at the desk. "Good luck."

After a bit Kim and Kurt came to a candy shop.

"That's the place to get a job!" Kurt said cheerfully.

"If I can't get a job, I can at least get a cavity," said Kim. She went in and got some sweets for herself and Kurt. Then she and Kurt flopped down on a bench.

Kim was hot and tired. She was starting to think she might never find a job. She sighed and set her chin on her hand.

"Don't be so gloomy," Kurt said. "You know what mom says: a quitter never wins, and a winner never quits."

Kim smiled. "You are right, Kurt. Thanks for saying that," she said. "I'll keep trying."

The Grocery

Not far from the shops Kim had just visited, Kurt spotted a big grocery store.

"Look!" Kurt exclaimed. "There is a poster on the window, Kim. It says 'Job Opening'."

Kim went inside and asked to speak to the boss.

"Hi, I'm Kim and this is Kurt. We saw your Job Opening ad in the window."

"Nice to meet you," said the grocer. "My name is Mr. Fremont. I own this grocery store."

Mr. Fremont was a large, jolly-looking man. Kim liked the look of him. She had a feeling he would be a kind boss.

"Have you ever had a job?" asked Mr. Fremont.

"No," said Kim. "But I can sweep and I can mop. I can help unpack boxes. I'm good at math, so I can help with the cash register. Just show me what to do!"

Mr. Fremont smiled.

"Well, Jeannie here is helping me take inventory at the moment," he said.

"What sort of food is inventory?" asked Kurt. "Is it yummy?"

Mr. Fremont was going to reply, but Kim cut in. "Inventory is not a food, you silly goof. Inventory means they are counting all the goods in the shop. They need to know precisely how many of each item they have. Then they will know how many they need to order."

"It sounds like you know a lot about how to run a grocery store," said Mr. Fremont.

"I know some," Kim said cheerfully. "You can teach me the rest quickly. I'm good with details and problem solving."

"Well, Miss Kim," said Mr. Fremont, "I have taken a liking to you. You seem bright. But would you mind if I gave you one or two tests to see what you can do?"

"No problem!" Kim said.

"I would like a job, too," Kurt said.

"And I would like to hire you," said Mr. Fremont. "But I can't. You are a child and the law says I can't hire children."

"Too bad," said Kurt. "I'm a good counter, too.

"I'll tell you what," Mr. Fremont said. "I have a small task for your sister. You watch her and let me know if she makes a mistake. Okay?"

"Okay," said Kurt.

Inventory

Mr. Fremont showed Kim how to take inventory. It seemed like it would be very easy to do.

"Just count the cans and write down the quantity for each one," said Mr. Fremont.

"What's quantity mean?" asked Kurt.

"A quantity is a number," Kim explained. "When you write down a quantity, you write down how many of the thing you have."

Kim counted the cans of peas. "One, two, three…"

"How many are there?" Kurt asked eagerly.

"Hush!" said Kim. "You made me lose count. I have to start over!"

Kim counted the cans of peas. Then she counted the cans of beans.

"There are so many kinds of beans!" Kurt said. "There must be a hundred kinds. I see baked beans, butter beans, pinto beans, green beans, white beans, and kidney beans."

Every time Kurt said something, Kim lost count.

"Kurt, I need some peace and quiet here, if you don't mind. This is not quite as easy as it looks. If you keep yapping, I will never get the quantities right."

Kurt sat quietly for a while and Kim counted everything carefully.

Kurt lay down on his tummy.

"Golly," he said, "somebody needs to sweep under these shelves. It's very dusty under there." He traced a smiley face in the dust.

"Hush, Kurt! If you will just sit there quietly, then I can count these cans and maybe we can go do something fun. I need to focus on the counting."

Kim counted cans of cherries and jars of jelly while Kurt sat quietly. At last, she finished.

"Let's go find Mr. Fremont," she said.

They found him at his desk.

"I saw Kim work, Mr. Fremont," Kurt said. "She counted everything carefully and I think she got the quan-ditty just right."

"Quantity," said Kim, "with a 't'."

Mr. Fremont looked at the numbers Kim had jotted down.

"You did a fine job!" he said. "I counted those cans before lunch today. So I know how many there are. Your count is the same as my count. That means you have passed this test! There is just one test left."

"OK," said Kim. "Let's do it!"

The Tally

Mr. Fremont led Kim to the cash register.

"Let's pretend you already have a job here," he said.

"Okay," said Kim.

Mr. Fremont went and got some things from the shelves and plopped them into a shopping basket. He selected a jar of peanut butter, a bag of cookies, and a key lime pie. Then he set the basket on the counter next to Kim.

"Can you tally up the cost of all this food?"

"You bet!" said Kim cheerfully. "Do you want me to use the cash register?"

"No," said Mr. Fremont. "I want to see if you can do it without the cash register. Let's pretend the cash register is broken. So you have to add up the tally all by yourself."

That sounded hard to Kurt. He looked at Kim to see if she looked scared. She did not.

"No problem," said Kim.

Kim got a sheet of paper and a pen. She wrote down the cost of each item. Then she added it up carefully.

When she finished she said, "Mr. Fremont, should I add the sales tax on top of this?"

Kurt looked at Mr. Fremont and saw him break into a big grin. Mr. Fremont's grin seemed to stretch from ear to ear. Kurt could not tell why he was so happy.

"Yes," Mr. Fremont said. "We must add in the sales tax."

"What is sales tax?" Kurt asked.

Mr. Fremont explained, "It's a tax we have to pay to the state to help pay for roads and firemen and that sort of thing."

Meanwhile Kim had finished adding in the tax. When she was finished, Mr. Fremont checked her numbers.

"Wow!" said Mr. Fremont. "You added and multiplied perfectly!"

He held out a hand for Kim to shake and said, "You've got yourself a job!"

"For real?" said Kim.

"For real!" said Mr. Fremont. "You can start next week."

Kurt clapped his hands.

"I'm so excited!" Kim said.

"Well, you should be proud of yourself," said Mr. Fremont. "It's never easy to find a job."

"You got that right!" Kurt said, sighing loudly. "It took us all day!"

"Just one day?" Mr. Fremont asked. "I'm impressed. Sometimes it takes a lot longer."

"I suppose I got lucky," replied Kim.

"Luck is finding a dime on the ground," Mr. Fremont said. "Getting a job is not luck. You had to visit a lot of places and talk to a lot of people. And you had to pass the tests I gave you."

Mr. Fremont showed Kim the rest of the store and the warehouse. Then he had her fill out some papers.

Mr. Fremont handed Kim twenty bucks for the time she had spent taking inventory and tallying up the costs. Then the two of them shook hands.

"Be here at nine o'clock sharp. Don't be late!"

"You can count on me, Mr. Fremont. I will be here, on time, every day."

Kim and Kurt went outside.

Kurt said, "Way to go, big sis!" They slapped hands and did a dance on the sidewalk.

Kim got out her cell phone and called her mom, who was at work.

"Mom," she said, "I got a job!"

"Whooooo-hooo!" said her mom.

The Visit

Kim was happy that she had found herself a summer job.

"Let's go and visit Mom," she said. "She will be finished teaching by the time we get there."

Mrs. Gunter was a math teacher. She taught at a college in lower Manhattan.

Kim held up a hand to hail a cab.

A yellow cab screeched to a stop on the side of the street. Kurt and Kim hopped in.

"Where to?" asked the driver.

Kim told him the address.

The cab went shooting off. Wind came rushing in the windows as the cab sped past stores on both sides.

Kurt hung on tight. It was a crazy ride. The cab man was weaving in and out of traffic. Kurt thought they might crash. Part of him was frightened. But part of him found driving at that speed exciting. It was like riding in a race car.

"Do you have a license to drive?" Kurt called to the driver.

"Yes. All cab drivers must have a license," the driver said.

"And they teach you to drive like this?"

"No, no," said the driver. "It takes years and years of driving to become an expert like me!"

They made it safely. Kim paid the driver and gave him a tip. She and Kurt went in to see their mom.

Mrs. Gunter gave Kim a big hug. Kurt snuck in between them so he could be part of the hug, too. Then Kim told her mom how they had spent the day.

Kim listed the places they had visited. She explained what had happened with Tom and Beth, with Alberto at the Corner Market, with Dwight, the Man of Light, with Hester the Florist, and, at last, with Mr. Fremont. She told her mom how she had used math to help her get the job at the grocery.

By the end of the story, Mrs. Gunter was beaming. "You see," she said. "I told you math would help you out one day. You thought I was crazy."

"You were right," said Kim. "Mr. Fremont was really impressed that I could add up the tally without the cash register and also add in the sales tax."

"Good for you!" said her mom. "I'm so proud of you!"

"I never dreamed I would have a job in a grocery," added Kim, "but I think it's going to be a good job for me."

"It may not be the job of your dreams," said her mom. "But it's a job. The next job you get can be better. And the next one can be even better. If you study hard in college, you will have a chance to get the job of your dreams some day. Until then, just do a good job and save as much of your paycheck as you can."

"I will," said Kim.

"Let's do something fun!" said Kurt.

"I know!" said their mom. "Let's celebrate Kim's new job by getting some subs and snacks and going down to Battery Park for a picnic. Are you two hungry for dinner?"

"You bet!" said Kurt.

"This is crazy!" Kim said. "Mom, all day, Kurt ate and ate. Each time I got him a snack, I said, that's the end of that. But he was still hungry."

"Well, he's a strong, growing child," said Mrs. Gunter. "And he was busy all day."

"That's right!" said Kurt.

They went to a sub shop nearby. Mrs. Gunter ordered a sub for each of them, plus some snacks and drinks.

Then Mrs. Gunter hailed a cab. The three of them got in. The cab took them down the West Side Highway. It dropped them off in Battery Park, on the south end of Manhattan.

Battery Park

As the sun went down, Mrs. Gunter, Kim, and Kurt had a picnic in Battery Park.

Kim was all set to relax. She was tired after her long day of job hunting.

After the picnic, Kurt went to the railing and pointed at the Statue of Liberty.

"Why is the Statue of Liberty holding up an ice cream cone?" he asked.

Kim smiled. "Kurt! That's not an ice cream cone! It's a torch!"

"What's a torch?"

"A torch is a stick with fire on one end," said Kim.

"Fire is cool!" said Kurt.

"A torch is what they used in the old days when there were no lights," Mrs. Gunter explained.

"I'll bet Dwight, the Man of Light sells torches!" said Kurt.

Kim smiled. "And since it's Dwight," she said, "I'll bet the price is right!"

Mrs. Gunter explained, "The Statue of Liberty was given to the United States by France."

"You mean it was a gift?" Kurt asked.

Mrs. Gunter nodded.

"Man," he said, "that's one big present! They must have needed a big box to gift wrap it."

"I think they sent it over here in parts and then welded the parts back together to make the statue."

"Welding is cool!" said Kurt.

"There are cooler things in life than welding," said Mrs. Gunter.

"Like what?" said Kurt.

"Like being free," said Mrs. Gunter. "People here in the United States are free. Mr. Fremont is free to hire Kim or not hire her. And Kim is free to take the job he offers her or not. Later on, if Kim decides to try to find a different job, she is free to do it. If we decide to pack up our stuff and leave Brooklyn, we are free to do it. Also, we are free to say what we feel like saying. That's what liberty means. It means being free to do what you wish, say what you wish, and think what you wish. Do you understand?"

Kurt nodded.

Mrs. Gunter went on, "The Statue of Liberty reminds us that we are free. It reminds us that liberty is a priceless thing."

Kurt looked back at the Statue of Liberty. He was thinking of all the things he was free to be when he got bigger: a baseball player, a shop owner, a banker, a baker, a race car driver, a spaceship driver.

"I see what you mean," he said. "Liberty is even cooler than welding."

Kurt helped Kim and his mom clean up the picnic. They tossed their trash into a trash can. Then they went to the subway stop to catch a train back to Brooklyn.

About this Book

This book has been created for use by students learning to read with the Core Knowledge Language Arts. Readability levels are suitable for early readers. The book has also been carefully leveled in terms of its "code load," or the number of spellings used in the stories.

The English writing system is complex. It uses more than 200 spellings to stand for 40-odd sounds. Many sounds can be spelled several different ways, and many spellings can be pronounced several different ways. This book has been designed to make early reading experiences easier and more productive by using a subset of the available spellings. It uses *only* spellings that students have been taught to sound out as part of their phonics lessons, plus a handful of tricky words, which have also been deliberately introduced in the lessons. This means that the stories will be 100% decodable if they are assigned at the proper time.

As the students move through the program, they learn new spellings and the "code load" in the decodable readers increases gradually. The code load graphics on this page indicate the number of spellings students are expected to know in order to read the first story of the book and the number of spellings students are expected to know in order to read the final stories in the book. The columns on the inside back cover list the specific spellings and tricky words students are expected to recognize at the beginning of this reader. The bullets at the bottom of the inside back cover identify spellings, tricky words, and other topics that are introduced gradually in the unit this reader is designed to accompany.

Visit us on the web at www.coreknowledge.org

Core Knowledge Language Arts

Series Editor-in-Chief
E. D. Hirsch, Jr.

President
Linda Bevilacqua

Editorial Staff
Carolyn Gosse, Senior Editor - Preschool
Khara Turnbull, Materials Development Manager
Michelle L. Warner, Senior Editor - Listening & Learning

Mick Anderson
Robin Blackshire
Maggie Buchanan
Paula Coyner
Sue Fulton
Sara Hunt
Erin Kist
Robin Luecke
Rosie McCormick
Cynthia Peng
Liz Pettit
Ellen Sadler
Deborah Samley
Diane Auger Smith
Sarah Zelinke

Design and Graphics Staff
Scott Ritchie, Creative Director

Kim Berrall
Michael Donegan
Liza Greene
Matt Leech
Bridget Moriarty
Lauren Pack

Consulting Project Management Services
ScribeConcepts.com

Additional Consulting Services
Ang Blanchette
Dorrit Green
Carolyn Pinkerton

Acknowledgments

These materials are the result of the work, advice, and encouragement of numerous individuals over many years. Some of those singled out here already know the depth of our gratitude; others may be surprised to find themselves thanked publicly for help they gave quietly and generously for the sake of the enterprise alone. To helpers named and unnamed we are deeply grateful.

Contributors to Earlier Versions of these Materials

Susan B. Albaugh, Kazuko Ashizawa, Nancy Braier, Kathryn M. Cummings, Michelle De Groot, Diana Espinal, Mary E. Forbes, Michael L. Ford, Ted Hirsch, Danielle Knecht, James K. Lee, Diane Henry Leipzig, Martha G. Mack, Liana Mahoney, Isabel McLean, Steve Morrison, Juliane K. Munson, Elizabeth B. Rasmussen, Laura Tortorelli, Rachael L. Shaw, Sivan B. Sherman, Miriam E. Vidaver, Catherine S. Whittington, Jeannette A. Williams

We would like to extend special recognition to Program Directors Matthew Davis and Souzanne Wright who were instrumental to the early development of this program.

Schools

We are truly grateful to the teachers, students, and administrators of the following schools for their willingness to field test these materials and for their invaluable advice: Capitol View Elementary, Challenge Foundation Academy (IN), Community Academy Public Charter School, Lake Lure Classical Academy, Lepanto Elementary School, New Holland Core Knowledge Academy, Paramount School of Excellence, Pioneer Challenge Foundation Academy, New York City PS 26R (The Carteret School), PS 30X (Wilton School), PS 50X (Clara Barton School), PS 96Q, PS 102X (Joseph O. Loretan), PS 104Q (The Bays Water), PS 214K (Michael Friedsam), PS 223Q (Lyndon B. Johnson School), PS 308K (Clara Cardwell), PS 333Q (Goldie Maple Academy), Sequoyah Elementary School, South Shore Charter Public School, Spartanburg Charter School, Steed Elementary School, Thomas Jefferson Classical Academy, Three Oaks Elementary, West Manor Elementary.

And a special thanks to the CKLA Pilot Coordinators Anita Henderson, Yasmin Lugo-Hernandez, and Susan Smith, whose suggestions and day-to-day support to teachers using these materials in their classrooms was critical.

CREDITS

WRITERS
Mike Ford

ILLUSTRATORS AND IMAGE SOURCES
All illustrations by Jed Henry